THE BOOK OF NIGHTMARES

THE BOOK OF NIGHTMARES

GALWAY KINNELL

19 · HOUGHTON MIFFLIN COMPANY BOSTON · 71

First Printing w

International Standard Book Number: 0–395–12097–7
Library of Congress Catalog Card Number: 71–134312
Printed in the United States of America

Parts of this book first appeared in the following
magazines: "Under the Maud Moon," sections 1–3
in *The New Yorker*, sections 4–7 in the *Iowa Review*; "The Hen Flower" in *Harper's*; "The Shoes
of Wandering," sections 1–4 and 7 in *Poetry*, sections 5 and 6 in the *Quarterly Review of Literature*;
"Dear Stranger Extant in Memory by the Blue
Juniata" in *kayak*; "In the Hotel of Lost Light" in
Field; "The Dead Shall Be Raised Incorruptible" in
Sumac; "Lastness," sections 1–3 in *The New Yorker*,
sections 4–7 in the *New American Review*.

To

MAUD and FERGUS

> But this, though: death,
> the whole of death, — even before life's begun,
> to hold it also gently, and be good:
> this is beyond description!

—Rilke

CONTENTS

I

UNDER THE MAUD MOON

1

On the path,
by this wet site
of old fires —
black ashes, black stones, where tramps
must have squatted down,
gnawing on stream water,
unhouseling themselves on cursed bread,
failing to get warm at a twigfire —

I stop,
gather wet wood,
cut dry shavings, and for her,
whose face
I held in my hands
a few hours, whom I gave back
only to keep holding the space where she was,

I light
a small fire in the rain.

The black
wood reddens, the deathwatches inside
begin running out of time, I can see
the dead, crossed limbs
longing again for the universe, I can hear
in the wet wood the snap
and re-snap of the same embrace being torn.

The raindrops trying
to put the fire out
fall into it and are
changed: the oath broken,
the oath sworn between earth and water, flesh and spirit, broken,
to be sworn again,
over and over, in the clouds, and to be broken again,
over and over, on earth.

2

I sit a moment
by the fire, in the rain, speak
a few words into its warmth —
stone saint smooth stone — and sing
one of the songs I used to croak
for my daughter, in her nightmares.

Somewhere out ahead of me
a black bear sits alone
on his hillside, nodding from side
to side. He sniffs
the blossom-smells, the rained earth,
finally he gets up,
eats a few flowers, trudges away,
his fur glistening
in the rain.

The singed grease streams
out of the words, the one
held note
remains — a love-note
twisting under my tongue, like the coyote's bark,
curving off, into a
howl.

3

A round-
cheeked girlchild comes awake
in her crib. The green
swaddlings tear open,
a filament or vestment
tears, the blue
flower opens.

And she who is born,
she who sings and cries,
she who begins the passage, her hair
sprouting out,
her gums budding for her first spring on earth,
the mist still clinging about
her face, puts
her hand
into her father's mouth, to take hold of
his song.

4

It is all over,
little one, the flipping
and overleaping, the watery
somersaulting alone in the oneness
under the hill, under
the old, lonely bellybutton
pushing forth again
in remembrance,
the drifting there furled in the dark,
pressing a knee or elbow
along a slippery wall, sculpting
the world with each thrash — the stream
of omphalos blood humming all about you.

5

Her head
enters the headhold
which starts sucking her forth: being itself
closes down all over her, gives her
into the shuddering
grip of departure, the slow,
agonized clenches making
the last molds of her life in the dark.

6

The black eye
opens, the pupil
droozed with black hairs
stops, the chakra
on top of the brain throbs a long moment in world light,

and she skids out on her face into light,
this peck
of stunned flesh
clotted with celestial cheesiness, glowing
with the astral violet
of the underlife. And as they cut

her tie to the darkness
she dies
a moment, turns blue as a coal,
the limbs shaking
as the memories rush out of them. When

they hang her up
by the feet, she sucks
air, screams
her first song — and turns rose,

the slow,
beating, featherless arms
already clutching at the emptiness.

7

When it was cold
on our hillside, and you cried
in the crib rocking
through the darkness, on wood
knifed down to the curve of the smile, a sadness
stranger than ours, all of it
flowing from the other world,

I used to come to you
and sit by you
and sing to you. You did not know,
and yet you will remember,
in the silent zones
of the brain, a specter, descendant
of the ghostly forefathers, singing
to you in the nighttime —
not the songs
of light said to wave
through the bright hair of angels,
but a blacker
rasping flowering on that tongue.

For when the Maud moon
glimmered in those first nights,
and the Archer lay
sucking the icy biestings of the cosmos,
in his crib of stars,

I had crept down
to riverbanks, their long rustle
of being and perishing, down to marshes

where the earth oozes up
in cold streaks, touching the world
with the underglimmer
of the beginning,
and there learned my only song.

And in the days
when you find yourself orphaned,
emptied
of all wind-singing, of light,
the pieces of cursed bread on your tongue,

may there come back to you
a voice,
spectral, calling you
sister!
from everything that dies.

And then
you shall open
this book, even if it is the book of nightmares.

II

THE HEN FLOWER

1

Sprawled
on our faces in the spring
nights, teeth
biting down on hen feathers, bits of the hen
still stuck in the crevices — if only
we could let go
like her, throw ourselves
on the mercy of darkness, like the hen,

tuck our head
under a wing, hold ourselves still
a few moments, as she
falls out into her little trance in the witchgrass,
or turn over
and be stroked with a finger
down the throat feathers,
down the throat knuckles,
down over the hum
of the wishbone tuning its high D in thin blood,
down over
the breastbone risen up
out of breast flesh, until the fatted thing
woozes off, head
thrown back
on the chopping block, longing only
to die.

2

When the ax-
scented breeze flourishes
about her, her cheeks crush in,
her comb
grays, the gizzard
that turns the thousand acidic millstones of her fate
convulses: ready or not
the next egg, bobbling
its globe of golden earth,
skids forth, ridding her even
of the life to come.

3

Almost high
on subsided gravity, I remain afoot,
a hen flower
dangling from a hand,
wing
of my wing,
of my bones and veins,
of my flesh
hairs lifting all over me in the first ghostly breeze
after death,

wing
made only to fly — unable
to write out the sorrows of being unable
to hold another in one's arms — and unable
to fly,
and waiting, therefore,
for the sweet, eventual blaze in the genes,
that one day, according to gospel, shall carry it back
into pink skies, where geese

cross at twilight, honking
in tongues.

4

I have glimpsed
by corpse-light, in the opened cadaver
of hen, the mass of tiny,
unborn eggs, each getting
tinier and yellower as it reaches back toward
the icy pulp
of what is, I have felt the zero
freeze itself around the finger dipped slowly in.

5

When the Northern Lights
were opening across the black sky and vanishing,
lighting themselves up
so completely they were vanishing,
I put to my eye the lucent
section of the spealbone of a ram —

I thought suddenly
I could read the cosmos spelling itself,
the huge broken letters
shuddering across the black sky and vanishing,

and in a moment,
in the twinkling of an eye, it came to me
the mockingbird would sing all her nights the cry of the rifle,
the tree would hold the bones of the sniper who chose not to
    climb down,
the rose would bloom no one would see it,
the chameleon longing to be changed would remain the color
    of blood.

And I went up
to the henhouse, and took up
the hen killed by weasels, and lugged
the sucked
carcass into first light. And when I hoisted
her up among the young pines, a last
rubbery egg slipping out as I flung her high, didn't it happen
the dead
wings creaked open as she soared
across the arms of the Bear?

6

Sprawled face down, waiting
for the rooster to groan out
it is the empty morning, as he groaned out thrice
for the disciple
of stone,
he who crushed with his heel the brain out of the snake,

I remember long ago I sowed
my own first milk
tooth under hen feathers, I planted under hen feathers
the hook
of the wishbone,
which had broken itself so lovingly toward me.

For the future.

It has come to this.

7

Listen, Kinnell,
dumped alive
and dying into the old sway bed,
a layer of crushed feathers all that there is

between you
and the long shaft of darkness shaped as you,
let go.

Even this haunted room
all its materials photographed with tragedy,
even the tiny crucifix drifting face down at the center of the earth,
even these feathers freed from their wings forever
are afraid.

III

THE SHOES OF WANDERING

1

Squatting at the rack
in the Store of the Salvation
Army, putting on, one after one,
these shoes strangers have died from, I discover
the eldershoes of my feet,
that take my feet
as their first feet, clinging
down to the least knuckle and corn.

And I walk out now,
in dead shoes, in the new light,
on the steppingstones
of someone else's wandering,
a twinge
in this foot or that saying
turn or *stay* or *take*
forty-three giant steps
backwards, frightened
I may already have lost
the way: *the first step*, the Crone
who scried the crystal said, *shall be*
to lose the way.

2

Back at the Xvarna Hotel, I leave
unlocked the door jimmied over and over,

I draw the one,
lightning-tracked blind
in the narrow room under the freeway, I put off
the shoes, set them
side by side
by the bedside, curl
up on bedclothes gone stiff
from love-acid, night-sweat, gnash-dust
of tooth, and lapse back
into darkness.

3

A faint,
creaking noise
starts up in the room,
low-passing wing-
beats, or great, labored breath-takings
of somebody lungsore or old.

And the old
footsmells in the shoes, touched
back to life by my footsweats, as by
a child's kisses, rise,
drift up where I lie
self-hugged on the bedclothes, slide
down the flues
of dozed, beating hairs, and I can groan

or wheeze, it will be
the groan or wheeze of another — the elderfoot
of these shoes, the drunk
who died in this room, whose dream-child
might have got a laugh
out of those clenched, corned feet, putting
huge, comical kisses on them
through the socks, or a brother

shipped back burned
from the burning of Asians, sweating
his nightmare out to the end
in some whitewashed warehouse
for dying — the groan
or wheeze of one
who lays bare his errors by a harsher light,
his self-mutterings worse
than the farts, grunts, and belches
of an Oklahoma men's room,
as I shudder down to his nightmare.

4

The witness trees
blaze themselves a last time: the road
trembles as it starts across
swampland streaked with shined water, a lethe-
wind of chill air touches
me all over my body,
certain brain cells crackle like softwood in a great fire
or die,
each step a shock,
a shattering underfoot of mirrors sick of the itch
of our face-bones under their skins,
as memory reaches out
and lays bloody hands on the future, the haunted
shoes rising and falling
through the dust, wings of dust
lifting around them, as they flap
down the brainwaves of the temporal road.

5

Is it the foot,
which rubs the cobblestones
and snakestones all its days, this lowliest

of tongues, whose lick-tracks tell
our history of errors to the dust behind,
which is the last trace in us
of wings?

And is it
the hen's nightmare, or her secret dream,
to scratch the ground forever
eating the minutes out of the grains of sand?

6

On this road
on which I do not know how to ask for bread,
on which I do not know how to ask for water,
this path
inventing itself
through jungles of burnt flesh, ground of ground
bones, crossing itself
at the odor of blood, and stumbling on,

I long for the mantle
of the great wanderers, who lighted
their steps by the lamp
of pure hunger and pure thirst,

and whichever way they lurched was the way.

7

But when the Crone
held up my crystal skull to the moon,
when she passed my shoulder bones
across the Aquarian stars, she said:

*You live
under the Sign*

of the Bear, who flounders through chaos
in his starry blubber:
poor fool,
poor forked branch
of applewood, you will feel all your bones
break
over the holy waters you will never drink.

IV

DEAR STRANGER
EXTANT IN MEMORY BY THE BLUE JUNIATA

1

Having given up
on the deskman passed out
under his clock, who was to have banged
it is morning
on the police-locked, sheetmetal door,

I can hear the chime
of the Old Tower, tinny sacring-bell drifting out
over the city — chyme
of our loves
the peristalsis of the will to love forever
drives down, grain
after grain, into the last,
coldest room, which is memory —

and listen for the maggots
inhabiting beds old men have died in
to crawl out,
to break into the brain and cut
the nerves which keep the book of solitude.

2

Dear Galway,
   It began late one April night when I couldn't sleep. It was the
dark of the moon. My hand felt numb, the pencil went over the page
drawn on its way by I don't know what. It drew circles and figure-

eights and mandalas. I cried. I had to drop the pencil. I was shaking. I went to bed and tried to pray. At last I relaxed. Then I felt my mouth open. My tongue moved, my breath wasn't my own. The whisper which forced itself through my teeth said, *Virginia, your eyes shine back to me from my own world.* O God, I thought. My breath came short, my heart opened. O God I thought, now I have a demon lover.

Yours, faithless to this life,
Virginia

3

At dusk, by the blue Juniata —
"a rural America," the magazine said,
"now vanished, but extant in memory,
a primal garden lost forever . . ."
("You see," I told Mama, "we just *think* we're here . . .") —
the root-hunters
go out into the woods, pull up
love-roots from the virginal glades, bend
the stalks over shovel-handles
and lever them up, the huge,
bass, final
thrump
as each root unclutches from its spot.

4

Take kettle
of blue water.
Boil over twigfire
of ash wood. Grind root.
Throw in. Let macerate. Reheat
over ash ashes. Bottle.
Stopper with thumb
of dead man. Ripen
forty days in horse dung

in the wilderness. Drink.
Sleep.

And when you rise —
if you do rise — it will be in the sothic year
made of the raised salvages
of the fragments all unaccomplished
of years past, scraps
and jettisons of time mortality
could not grind down into his meal of blood and laughter.

And if there is one more love
to be known, one more poem
to be opened into life,
you will find it here
or nowhere. Your hand will move
on its own
down the curving path, drawn
down by the terror and terrible lure
of vacuum:

a face materializes into your hands,
on the absolute whiteness of pages
a poem writes itself out: its title — the dream
of all poems and the text
of all loves — "Tenderness toward Existence."

5

On this bank — our bank —
of the blue, vanished water, you lie,
crying in your bed, hearing those
small,
fearsome thrumps
of leave-taking trespassing the virginal woods at dusk.

I, too, have eaten
the meals of the dark shore. In time's

own mattress, where a sag shaped as a body
lies next to a sag — graves
tossed into it
by those who came before,
lovers,
or loving friends,
or strangers,
who loved here,
or ground their nightmared teeth here,
or talked away their one-night stands,
the sanctus-bell
going out each hour to die against the sheetglass city —

I lie without sleeping, remembering
the ripped body
of hen, the warmth of hen flesh
frightening my hand,
all her desires,
all her deathsmells,
blooming again in the starlight. And then the wait —

not long, I grant, but all my life —
for the small, soft
thud of her return among the stones.

Can it ever be true —
all bodies, one body, one light
made of everyone's darkness together?

6

Dear Galway,

I have no one to turn to because God is my enemy. He gave me
lust and joy and cut off my hands. My brain is smothered with his
blood. I asked why should I love this body I fear. He said, *It is so
lordly, it can never be shaped again — dear, shining casket. Have
you never been so proud of a thing you wanted it for your prey?*

His voice chokes my throat. Soul of asps, master and taker: he
wants to kill me. Forgive my blindness.

Yours, in the darkness,
Virginia

7

Dear stranger
extant in memory by the blue Juniata,
these letters
across space I guess
will be all we will know of one another.

So little of what one is threads itself through the eye
of empty space.

Never mind.
The self is the least of it.
Let our scars fall in love.

V

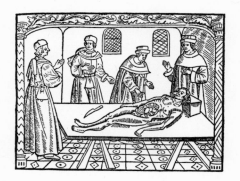

IN THE HOTEL OF LOST LIGHT

1

In the left-
hand sag the drunk smelling of autopsies
died in, my body slumped out
into the shape of his, I watch, as he
must have watched, a fly
tangled in mouth-glue, whining his wings,
concentrated wholly on
time, time, losing his way worse
down the downward-winding stairs, his wings
whining for life as he shrivels
in the gaze
from the spider's clasped forebrains, the abstracted stare
in which even the nightmare spatters out its horrors
and dies.

Now the fly
ceases to struggle, his wings
flutter out the music blooming with failure
of one who gets ready to die, as Roland's horn, winding down
from the Pyrenees, saved its dark, full flourishes
for last.

2

In the light
left behind by the little
spiders of blood who garbled

their memoirs across his shoulders
and chest, the room
echoes with the tiny thrumps
of crotch hairs plucking themselves
from their spots; on the stripped skin
the love-sick crab lice
struggle to unstick themselves and sprint from the doomed
    position —

and stop,
heads buried
for one last taste of the love-flesh.

3

Flesh
of his excavated flesh,
fill of his emptiness,
after-amanuensis of his after-life,
I write out
for him in this languished alphabet
of worms, these last words
of himself, post for him
his final postcards to posterity.

4

"I sat out by twigfires flaring in grease strewn from the pimpled limbs
    of hen,
I blacked out into oblivion by that crack in the curb where the forget-
    me blooms,
I saw the ferris wheel writing its huge, desolate zeroes in neon on the
    evening skies,
I painted my footsoles purple for the day when the beautiful color
    would show,
I staggered death-sentences down empty streets, the cobblestones as-
    sured me, *it shall be so,*

I heard my own cries already howled inside bottles the waves washed
    up on beaches,
I ghostwrote my prayers myself in the body-Arabic of these night-
    mares.

"If the deskman knocks, griping again
about the sweet, excremental
odor of opened cadaver creeping out
from under the door, tell him, 'Friend, *To Live*
has a poor cousin,
who calls tonight, who pronounces the family name
To Leave, she
changes each visit the flesh-rags on her bones.' "

5

Violet bruises come out
all over his flesh, as invisible
fists start beating him a last time; the whine
of omphalos blood starts up again, the puffed
bellybutton explodes, the carnal
nightmare soars back to the beginning.

6

As for the bones to be tossed
into the aceldama back of the potting shop, among
shards and lumps
which caught vertigo and sagged away
into mud, or crawled out of fire
crazed or exploded, they shall re-arise
in the pear tree, in spring, to shine down
on two clasping what they dream is one another.

As for these words scattered into the future —
posterity
is one invented too deep in its past
to hear them.

7

The foregoing scribed down
in March, of the year Seventy,
on my sixteen-thousandth night of war and madness,
in the Hotel of Lost Light, under the freeway
which roams out into the dark
of the moon, in the absolute spell
of departure, and by the light
from the joined hemispheres of the spider's eyes.

VI

THE DEAD SHALL
BE RAISED INCORRUPTIBLE

1

A piece of flesh gives off
smoke in the field —

carrion,
caput mortuum,
orts,
pelf,
fenks,
sordes,
gurry dumped from hospital trashcans.

Lieutenant!
This corpse will not stop burning!

2

"That you Captain? Sure,
sure I remember — I still hear you
lecturing at me on the intercom, *Keep your guns up, Burnsie!*
and then screaming, *Stop shooting, for crissake, Burnsie,*
those are friendlies! But crissake, Captain,
I'd already started, burst
after burst, little black pajamas jumping
and falling . . . and remember that pilot
who'd bailed out over the North,
how I shredded him down to catgut on his strings?
one of his slant eyes, a piece

of his smile, sail past me
every night right after the sleeping pill . . .

"It was only
that I loved the *sound*
of them, I guess I just loved
the *feel* of them sparkin' off my hands . . ."

3

On the television screen:

Do you have a body that sweats?
Sweat that has odor?
False teeth clanging into your breakfast?
Case of the dread?
Headache so perpetual it may outlive you?
Armpits sprouting hair?
Piles so huge you don't need a chair to sit at a table?

We shall not all sleep, but we shall be changed . . .

4

In the Twentieth Century of my trespass on earth,
having exterminated one billion heathens,
heretics, Jews, Moslems, witches, mystical seekers,
black men, Asians, and Christian brothers,
every one of them for his own good,

a whole continent of red men for living in unnatural community
and at the same time having relations with the land,
one billion species of animals for being sub-human,
and ready to take on the bloodthirsty creatures from the other
      planets,
I, Christian man, groan out this testament of my last will.

I give my blood fifty parts polystyrene,
twenty-five parts benzene, twenty-five parts good old gasoline,
to the last bomber pilot aloft, that there shall be one acre
in the dull world where the kissing flower may bloom,
which kisses you so long your bones explode under its lips.

My tongue goes to the Secretary of the Dead
to tell the corpses, "I'm sorry, fellows,
the killing was just one of those things
difficult to pre-visualize — like a cow,
say, getting hit by lightning."

My stomach, which has digested
four hundred treaties giving the Indians
eternal right to their land, I give to the Indians,
I throw in my lungs which have spent four hundred years
sucking in good faith on peace pipes.

My soul I leave to the bee
that he may sting it and die, my brain
to the fly, his back the hysterical green color of slime,
that he may suck on it and die, my flesh to the advertising man,
the anti-prostitute, who loathes human flesh for money.

I assign my crooked backbone
to the dice maker, to chop up into dice,
for casting lots as to who shall see his own blood
on his shirt front and who his brother's,
for the race isn't to the swift but to the crooked.

To the last man surviving on earth
I give my eyelids worn out by fear, to wear
in his long nights of radiation and silence,
so that his eyes can't close, for regret
is like tears seeping through closed eyelids.

I give the emptiness my hand: the pinkie picks no more noses,
slag clings to the black stick of the ring finger,

a bit of flame jets from the tip of the fuck-you finger,
the first finger accuses the heart, which has vanished,
on the thumb stump wisps of smoke ask a ride into the emptiness.

In the Twentieth Century of my nightmare
on earth, I swear on my chromium testicles
to this testament
and last will
of my iron will, my fear of love, my itch for money, and my
     madness.

5

In the ditch
snakes crawl cool paths
over the rotted thigh, the toe bones
twitch in the smell of burnt rubber,
the belly
opens like a poison nightflower,
the tongue has evaporated,
the nostril
hairs sprinkle themselves with yellowish-white dust,
the five flames at the end
of each hand have gone out, a mosquito
sips a last meal from this plate of serenity.

And the fly,
the last nightmare, hatches himself.

6

I ran
my neck broken I ran
holding my head up with both hands I ran
thinking the flames
the flames may burn the oboe
but listen buddy boy they can't touch the notes!

7

A few bones
lie about in the smoke of bones.

Membranes,
effigies pressed into grass,
mummy windings,
desquamations,
sags incinerated mattresses gave back to the world,
memories left in mirrors on whorehouse ceilings,
angel's wings
flagged down into the snows of yesteryear,

kneel
on the scorched earth
in the shapes of men and animals:

do not let this last hour pass,
do not remove this last, poison cup from our lips.

And a wind holding
the cries of love-making from all our nights and days
moves among the stones, hunting
for two twined skeletons to blow its last cry across.

Lieutenant!
This corpse will not stop burning!

VII

LITTLE SLEEP'S-HEAD
SPROUTING HAIR IN THE MOONLIGHT

1

You scream, waking from a nightmare.

When I sleepwalk
into your room, and pick you up,
and hold you up in the moonlight, you cling to me
hard,
as if clinging could save us. I think
you think
I will never die, I think I exude
to you the permanence of smoke or stars,
even as
my broken arms heal themselves around you.

2

I have heard you tell
the sun, *don't go down*, I have stood by
as you told the flower, *don't grow old*,
don't die. Little Maud,

I would blow the flame out of your silver cup,
I would suck the rot from your fingernail,
I would brush your sprouting hair of the dying light,
I would scrape the rust off your ivory bones,
I would help death escape through the little ribs of your body,
I would alchemize the ashes of your cradle back into wood,
I would let nothing of you go, ever,

until washerwomen
feel the clothes fall asleep in their hands,
and hens scratch their spell across hatchet blades,
and rats walk away from the cultures of the plague,
and iron twists weapons toward the true north,
and grease refuses to slide in the machinery of progress,
and men feel as free on earth as fleas on the bodies of men,
and lovers no longer whisper to the presence beside them in the
    dark, O *corpse-to-be* . . .

And yet perhaps this is the reason you cry,
this the nightmare you wake screaming from:
being forever
in the pre-trembling of a house that falls.

3

In a restaurant once, everyone
quietly eating, you clambered up
on my lap: to all
the mouthfuls rising toward
all the mouths, at the top of your voice
you cried
your one word, *caca! caca! caca!*
and each spoonful
stopped, a moment, in midair, in its withering
steam.

Yes,
you cling because
I, like you, only sooner
than you, will go down
the path of vanished alphabets,
the roadlessness
to the other side of the darkness,

your arms
like the shoes left behind,
like the adjectives in the halting speech
of old men,
which once could call up the lost nouns.

4

And you yourself,
some impossible Tuesday
in the year Two Thousand and Nine, will walk out
among the black stones
of the field, in the rain,

and the stones saying
over their one word, *ci-gît, ci-gît, ci-gît,*

and the raindrops
hitting you on the fontanel
over and over, and you standing there
unable to let them in.

5

If one day it happens
you find yourself with someone you love
in a café at one end
of the Pont Mirabeau, at the zinc bar
where white wine stands in upward opening glasses,

and if you commit then, as we did, the error
of thinking,
one day all this will only be memory,

learn,
as you stand
at this end of the bridge which arcs,

from love, you think, into enduring love,
learn to reach deeper
into the sorrows
to come — to touch
the almost imaginary bones
under the face, to hear under the laughter
the wind crying across the black stones. Kiss
the mouth
which tells you, *here*,
here is the world. This mouth. This laughter. These temple bones.

The still undanced cadence of vanishing.

6

In the light the moon
sends back, I can see in your eyes

the hand that waved once
in my father's eyes, a tiny kite
wobbling far up in the twilight of his last look:

and the angel
of all mortal things lets go the string.

7

Back you go, into your crib.

The last blackbird lights up his gold wings: *farewell.*
Your eyes close inside your head,
in sleep. Already
in your dreams the hours begin to sing.

Little sleep's-head sprouting hair in the moonlight,
when I come back
we will go out together,

we will walk out together among
the ten thousand things,
each scratched too late with such knowledge, *the wages
of dying is love.*

VIII

THE CALL ACROSS
THE VALLEY OF NOT-KNOWING

1

In the red house sinking down
into ground rot, a lamp
at one window, the smarled ashes letting
a single flame go free,
a shoe of dreaming iron nailed to the wall,
two mismatched halfnesses lying side by side in the darkness
I can feel with my hand
the foetus rouse himself
with a huge, fishy thrash, and re-settle in his darkness.

Her hair glowing in the firelight,
her breasts full,
her belly swollen,
a sunset of firelight
wavering all down one side, my wife sleeps on,
happy,
far away, in some other,
newly opened room of the world.

2

Sweat breaking from his temples,
Aristophanes ran off
at the mouth — made it all up, nightmared it all up
on the spur
of that moment which has stabbed us ever since:
that each of us

is a torn half
whose lost other we keep seeking across time
until we die, or give up —
or actually find her:

as I myself, in an Ozark
Airlines DC–6 droning over
towns made of crossroads, headed down
into Waterloo, Iowa, actually found her,
held her face a few hours
in my hands; and for reasons — cowardice,
loyalties, all which goes by the name "necessity" —
left her . . .

3

And yet I think
it must be the wound, the wound itself,
which lets us know and love,
which forces us to reach out to our misfit
and by a kind
of poetry of the soul, accomplish,
for a moment, the wholeness the drunk Greek
extrapolated from his high
or flagellated out of an empty heart,

that purest,
most tragic concumbence, strangers
clasped into one, a moment, of their moment on earth.

4

She who lies halved
beside me — she and I once
watched the bees, dreamers not yet
dipped into the acids
of the craving for anything, not yet burned down into flies, sucking
the blossom-dust
from the pear-tree in spring,

we two
lay out together
under the tree, on earth, beside our empty clothes,
our bodies opened to the sky,
and the blossoms glittering in the sky
floated down
and the bees glittered in the blossoms
and the bodies of our hearts
opened
under the knowledge
of tree, on the grass of the knowledge
of graves, and among the flowers of the flowers.

And the brain kept blossoming
all through the body, until the bones themselves could think,
and the genitals sent out wave after wave of holy desire
until even the dead brain cells
surged and fell in god-like, androgynous fantasies —
and I understood
the unicorn's phallus could have risen, after all,
directly out of thought itself.

5

Of that time in a Southern jail,
when the sheriff, as he cursed me
and spat, took my hand in his hand, rocked
from the pulps the whorls
and tented archways into the tabooed realm, that underlife
where the canaries of the blood are singing, pressed
the flesh-flowers
into the dirty book of the
police-blotter, afterwards what I remembered most
was the care, the almost loving,
animal gentleness of his hand on my hand.

Better than the rest of us, he knows
the harshness of that cubicle

in hell where they put you
with all your desires undiminished, and with no body to appease
    them.

And when he himself floats out
on a sea he almost begins to remember,
floats out into a darkness he has known already;
when the moan of wind
and the gasp of lungs call to each other among the waves
and the wish to float
comes to matter not at all as he sinks under,

is it so impossible to think
he will dream back to all hands black and white
he took in his hands
as the creation
touches him a last time all over his body?

6

Suppose I had stayed
with that woman of Waterloo, suppose
we had met on a hill called Safa, in our own country,
that we had lain out on the grass
and looked into each other's blindness, under leaf-shadows
wavering across our bodies in the drifts of sun,
our faces
inclined toward each other, as hens
incline their faces
when the heat flows from the warmed egg
back into the whole being, and the silver moon
had stood still for us in the middle of heaven —

I think I might have closed my eyes, and moved
from then on like the born blind,
their faces
gone into heaven already.

7

We who live out our plain lives, who put
our hand into the hand of whatever we love
as it vanishes,
as we vanish,
and stumble toward what will be, simply by arriving,
a kind of fate,

some field, maybe, of flaked stone
scattered in starlight
where the flesh
swaddles its skeleton a last time
before the bones go their way without us,

might we not hear, even then,
the bear call
from his hillside — a call, like ours, needing
to be answered — and the dam-bear
call back across the darkness
of the valley of not-knowing
the only word tongues shape without intercession,

yes . . . yes . . . ?

IX

THE PATH AMONG THE STONES

On the path winding
upward, toward the high valley
of waterfalls and flooded, hoof-shattered
meadows of spring,
where fish-roots boil
in the last grails of light on the water,
and vipers pimpled with urges to fly
drape the black stones hissing *pheet! pheet!* — land
of quills
and inkwells of skulls filled with black water —

I come to a field
glittering with the thousand sloughed skins
of arrowheads, stones
which shuddered and leapt forth
to give themselves into the broken hearts
of the living,
who gave themselves back, broken, to the stone.

2

I close my eyes:
on the heat-rippled beaches
where the hills came down to the sea,
the luminous
beach dust pounded out of funeral shells,
I can see

them living without me, dying
without me, the wing
and egg
shaped stones, broken
war-shells of slain fighting conches,
dog-eared immortality shells
in which huge constellations of slime, by the full moon,
writhed one more
coat of invisibility on a speck of sand,

and the agates knocked
from circles scratched into the dust
with the click
of a wishbone breaking, inward-swirling
globes biopsied out of sunsets never to open again,

and that wafer-stone
which skipped ten times across
the water, suddenly starting to run as it went under,
and the zeroes it left,
that met
and passed into each other, they themselves
smoothing themselves from the water . . .

3

I walk out from myself,
among the stones of the field,
each sending up its ghost-bloom
into the starlight, to float out
over the trees, seeking to be one
with the unearthly fires kindling and dying

in space — and falling back, knowing
the sadness of the wish
to alight
back among the glitter of bruised ground,

the stones holding between pasture and field,
the great, granite nuclei,
glimmering, even they, with ancient inklings of madness and war.

4

A way opens
at my feet. I go down
the night-lighted mule-steps into the earth,
the footprints behind me
filling already with pre-sacrificial trills
of canaries, go down
into the unbreathable goaf
of everything I ever craved and lost.

An old man, a stone
lamp at his forehead, squats
by his hell-flames, stirs into
his pot
chopped head
of crow, strings of white light,
opened tail of peacock, dressed
body of canary, robin breast
dragged through the mud of battlefields, wrung-out
blossom of caput mortuum flower — salts
it all down with sand
stolen from the upper bells of hourglasses . . .

Nothing.
Always nothing. Ordinary blood
boiling away in the glare of the brow lamp.

5

And yet, no,
perhaps not nothing. Perhaps
not ever nothing. In clothes

woven out of the blue spittle
of snakes, I crawl up: I find myself alive
in the whorled
archway of the fingerprint of all things,
skeleton groaning,
blood-strings wailing the wail of all things.

6

The witness trees heal
their scars at the flesh fire,
the flame
rises off the bones,
the hunger
to be new lifts off
my soul, an eerie blue light blooms
on all the ridges of the world. Somewhere
in the legends of blood sacrifice
the fatted calf
takes the bonfire into his arms, and *he*
burns *it*.

7

As above: the last scattered stars
kneel down in the star-form of the Aquarian age:
a splash
on the top of the head,
on the grass of this earth even the stars love, splashes of the
    sacred waters . . .

So below: in the graveyard
the lamps start lighting up, one for each of us,
in all the windows
of stone.

X

LASTNESS

1

The skinny waterfalls, footpaths
wandering out of heaven, strike
the cliffside, leap, and shudder off.

Somewhere behind me
a small fire goes on flaring in the rain, in the desolate ashes.
No matter, now, whom it was built for,
it keeps its flames,
it warms
everyone who might wander into its radiance,
a tree, a lost animal, the stones,

because in the dying world it was set burning.

2

A black bear sits alone
in the twilight, nodding from side
to side, turning slowly around and around
on himself, scuffing the four-footed
circle into the earth. He sniffs the sweat
in the breeze, he understands
a creature, a death-creature
watches from the fringe of the trees,
finally he understands
I am no longer here, he himself
from the fringe of the trees watches

a black bear
get up, eat a few flowers, trudge away,
all his fur glistening
in the rain.

And what glistening! Sancho Fergus,
my boychild, had such great shoulders,
when he was born his head
came out, the rest of him stuck. And he opened
his eyes: his head out there all alone
in the room, he squinted with pained,
barely unglued eyes at the ninth-month's
blood splashing beneath him
on the floor. And almost
smiled, I thought, almost forgave it all in advance.

When he came wholly forth
I took him up in my hands and bent
over and smelled
the black, glistening fur
of his head, as empty space
must have bent
over the newborn planet
and smelled the grasslands and the ferns.

3

Walking toward the cliff, I call out
to the stone,
and the stone
calls back, its voice hunting among the rubble
for my ears.

Stop.
As you approach an echoing
cliffside, you sense the line
where the voice calling from stone

no longer answers,
turns into stone, and nothing comes back.

Here, between answer
and nothing, I stand, in the old shoes
flowed over by rainbows of hen-oil,
each shoe holding the bones
which ripple together in the communion
of the step,
and which open out
in front into toes, the whole foot trying
to dissolve into the future.

A clatter of elk hooves.
Has the top sphere
emptied itself? Is it true
the earth is all there is, and the earth does not last?

On the river the world floats by holding one corpse.

Stop.
Stop here.
Living brings you to death, there is no other road.

4

This is the tenth poem
and it is the last. It is right
at the last, that one
and zero
walk off together,
walk off the end of these pages together,
one creature
walking away side by side with the emptiness.

Lastness
is brightness. It is the brightness

gathered up of all that went before. It lasts.
And when it does end
there is nothing, nothing
left,

in the rust of old cars,
in the hole torn open in the body of the Archer,
in river-mist smelling of the weariness of stones,
the dead lie,
empty, filled, at the beginning,

and the first
voice comes craving again out of their mouths.

5

That Bach concert I went to so long ago —
the chandeliered room
of ladies and gentlemen who would never die . . .
the voices go out,
the room becomes hushed,
the violinist
puts the irreversible sorrow of his face
into the opened palm
of the wood, the music begins:

a shower of rosin,
the bow-hairs listening down all their length
to the wail,
the sexual wail
of the back-alleys and blood strings we have lived
still crying,
still singing, from the sliced intestine
of cat.

6

This poem
if we shall call it that,
or concert of one
divided among himself,
this earthward gesture
of the sky-diver, the worms
on his back still spinning forth
and already gnawing away
the silks of his loves, who could have saved him,
this free floating of one
opening his arms into the attitude
of flight, as he obeys the necessity and falls . . .

7

Sancho Fergus! Don't cry!

Or else, cry.

On the body,
on the blued flesh, when it is
laid out, see if you can find
the one flea which is laughing.